This Book Will Teach You
How to Cook Healthy
AF with Minimal Effort

By Ariana Curcio

Copyright © 2021 by Ariana Curcio

All rights reserved. No part of this publication may be reproduced, stored in a retrieval system, or transmitted, in any form or by any means, electronic, mechanical, photocopying, recording, or otherwise, without the prior written permission of the publisher. Printed in The United States of America.

The information in this book is true and complete to the best of my knowledge. It is intended as an informative guide for people who wish to learn how to cook with ease and health in mind. It is in no way intended to replace, countermand or conflict with the advice given to you by a physician. Information in this book is general and offered with no guarantees on part of the author/publisher. The author/publisher disclaims all liability in connection with the use of this book.

First edition 2021

ABOUT THE AUTHOR
As a child of the '80s, I was constantly playing outside and riding my bike, until I turned 12 years old and came down with an intense form of Hyper Thyroidisim called Graves Disease. No exaggeration, I didn't sleep for a full year. I had so much energy from such a high-functioning metabolism that despite my horrible diet of sugary cereals and ice cream, I was rail-thin, and my eyes and thyroid gland bulged out of my body. What a sight I was!

After getting medical help, my body made drastic changes and did a complete 360. I now slept all the time and kept gaining weight, which was good until it wasn't. This was the beginning of figuring out a healthier way of eating, especially since I'm an Italian from N.Y. (no ketosis for me, thank you.)

Since then, I have spent years and years playing, experimenting, and joyfully cooking for friends and family, in the pursuit of healthier ways of preparing traditional dishes and comfort food (and to basically satiate my cravings!) There's no formal training here, no nutrition degrees and I don't claim to be an expert or know it all. I just know that this works for me and my family and I wholeheartedly love doing it. This is a reclamation of personal power, one non-dairy cream sauce at a time and I promise that it's easier than you think and honestly delicious.
If I can do it, you can too. So let's get cooking!

INTRODUCTION

We've all heard the excuses- I would eat healthier if I knew how to cook or I don't have the time to make healthy food or, my favorite one- healthy food is expensive and I can't afford it. BULLSHIT!
It's really not hard so stop making excuses. The truth is you are too lazy to eat healthier because you think it's hard to do and takes a lot of effort. You want convenient, fake-ass food, perhaps because that is what you grew up on, or you were deprived as a child and are trying to make up for the lost time. Whatever the reason, you're not doing yourself any favors. You're shortening your life, speeding up the aging process, taking too many antacids, and feeling sluggish.
There's no reason you can't get your shit together if you really want to. You don't have to deprive yourself of meat, dairy, gluten, or fat, but my god, you can limit, substitute and live by an EVERYTHING IN MODERATION way of life.

One of the worst things we can put in our bodies is preservatives. Cold cuts, canned meals, boxed mac and cheese, canned soups, etc. are LOADED with preservatives. There's even a brand of food that sells a complete line of 3-course meals that are stored on a shelf! A FULL ROAST DINNER ON A SHELF!!!! If we are in apocalyptic times, they may come in very handy, but until then, for the sake of your body- please don't engage in crap like that. This book will teach you how to cook, with minimal effort and tricks and tips for a lifetime of healthy eating without sacrificing taste and contentment, using minimal preservatives.

A few things to go over before we start doling out recipes here; first- invest in a slow cooker, air fryer (not the same thing as a convection oven, I swear), or an Insta Pot- they will change your life. With a coupon or a sale, you can purchase a very decent brand for a very affordable price. Comb social media marketplaces for unused ones that are victims of a moving sale or garage cleanout. If you feel nervous leaving a slow cooker on all day because of a fire hazard, get into the habit of drying out your kitchen sink and placing it in there for the day while it cooks (I read this tip from a fire department once and it makes a lot of sense.)

Bottom line- this book WILL teach you how to cook, healthy AF with minimal effort. Don't look for fancy photos- if you don't know what tomato sauce or chicken soup looks like, you have much bigger problems than eating preservatives. Also, if I have to tell you to add salt and pepper to your taste preference to all of these recipes you should probably hang up the apron now.

Basic Staples to Have on Hand
- Mirepoix — Page 11
- Cashew Cream — Page 11
- Broth/Stocks — Page 12
- Vegetable Broth — Page 12
- Chicken (or Beef or Fish) Stock — Page 13
- Chicken/Beef Broth — Page 13
- Other Staples to Have on Hand — Page 14

Soups
- Split Pea — Page 16
- Chicken Soup — Page 17
- Cream of Broccoli — Page 18
- Cream of Tomato — Page 19
- Minestrone — Page 20
- Italian Wedding — Page 22
- Lentil — Page 24
- Seafood Bisque — Page 25
- Butternut Squash — Page 26
- Ginger Lemongrass Mushroom — Page 27
- Clam Chowder (Red & White) — Page 28
- "Date Night" Soup — Page 30

Sauces
- Pomodoro/Meatballs — Page 34
- Vodka — Page 36
- Pumpkin — Page 38
- Clam — Page 39

Mains with Grains
- Mushroom Risotto — Page 42
- Cauliflower/Broccoli Pasta — Page 44
- Paella — Page 45

Meat Mains
    Escarole & Beans with Sausage   Page 50
    Chicken Variations   Page 51
    Chicken Cutlets   Page 52
    Shrimp   Page 53
    Italian Tuna   Page 54
    Chili   Page 55
    Pulled Chicken or Pork   Page 56

Vegetable Mains
    Eggplant   Page 58
    Zucchini/Eggplant Lasagna   Page 59
    Curry   Page 60

Stews
    Beef Stew   Page 64
    Turkey or Chicken Stew   Page 64
    White Bean Stew with Sausage   Page 65

Vegetables/Sides
    Creamed Spinach or Corn   Page 68
    Brussel Sprouts   Page 69
    Butternut Squash   Page 70
    Pasta Salad   Page 71
    Potato Salad   Page 73

Dessert   Page 74
Kitchen Hacks   Page 75

BASIC STAPLES TO HAVE ON HAND

MIREPOIX
So let's crawl out of under that rock and pay attention! Most dishes start with a base the French call Mirepoix- a mix of carrot, celery & onion (pronounced mear-pwoh for you ignoramuses.) You can save a lot of time by buying a premade Mirepoix and keep in the freezer for the ready!

If you don't have any you can make your own Mirepoix by doing this:
1 large yellow or white onion chopped
3-4 stalks of celery chopped
3-4 carrot sticks or approximately 15-20 baby carrots chopped

If my recipe states just the word "POIX" omit the carrots- they don't belong in everything- they know their place.

CASHEW CREAM
Make cashew cream a staple in your kitchen, it replaces dairy in recipes, no one will ever know, and you won't feel sick full. Dairy is not optimal for health and can make you fat, treat dairy as a TREAT because it's one.

You can buy shelved cashew cream, but it's so easy, it's almost a sin, and PRESERVATIVES!

Raw, unsalted cashews
Filtered water
That's it- see how effing easy it's to be healthy

Cover the cashews with water and leave them out overnight. The next day, drain and rinse the cashews. Puree in a blender or processor, adding filtered water a ¼ cup at a time until you get a cream-like consistency. Freeze in ½ cup batches to use in recipes in a pinch.

BROTH/STOCK

The difference between broth and stock is that stock is made from bones. Use broth in soups and stock in cooking liquids. Yes, it's easy enough to buy, but if you can save money and know what is in it, why wouldn't you? I turn to the carton when I haven't had enough stuff to make my own, but if you can, do so, and PLEASE splurge for the low sodium, organic stuff!

VEGETABLE BROTH

Save all of the remnants from your vegetables when you cook and freeze them as you go- the butts of the celery and carrots, the outer part of the onion, broccoli stalks, etc. in large freezer bags. Once you accumulate a bunch add them to your slow cooker with filtered water (4 hours on high or 8 hours on low) or boil on medium for an hour in a stockpot, strain, and use this liquid as your cooking broth. Discard/compost veggies.

CHICKEN STOCK (OR BEEF, OR FISH)
Take any bones from chicken, beef, or fish (don't mix, stick to one) while you eat or cook (think rotisserie, thighs, etc.) Once you accumulate a bunch add them to your slow cooker with filtered water (4 hours on high or 8 hours on low) or boil on medium for an hour in a stockpot, with mirepoix, parsley, bay leaves, and salt and pepper, strain and use this liquid as your cooking stock. Discard bones.

CHICKEN/BEEF BROTH
Essentially, boiling chicken or beef in water with mirepoix, parsley, and any other desired herbs will give you chicken or beef broth. You can eat that as soup or strain the liquid and use the boiled meat in an array of ways- chicken salad, pot pie, meat stuffing, the possibilities are endless.

DON'T SKIMP
Do you know why the food is so good at expensive restaurants? It's because they use high-quality ingredients (they also use copious amounts of butter/fat, which is why it's much healthier to cook for yourself). But that isn't the objective of this paragraph. The point of this section is this; spend money on the higher quality ingredients such as butter, olive oils, spices, herbs, flours, etc. These are the base of your

meals and will make all the difference in taste. We get so attracted by saving 30 cents and coupons/sales that we lose sight of what is more important. Quality!
For example, when I state grated Romano cheese in my recipes, I am using high-quality grated cheese from a pork store, not from a supermarket shelf. It is not packaged in a tin can, but rather a plastic bag or tub. It makes a world of difference. If you are on a budget, use a tad bit smaller portion than you normally would, it is a life-changer. Skimp on other things like paper towels or counter spray (make your own with vinegar and water).

Other staples to always have on hand:
Olive oil (extra virgin for raw foods, regular for cooking)
Canned tomatoes (organic, cheap ass)
Broths and stocks
Pasta, Beans, Lentils, and Grains
Frozen Vegetables, Seafood, and Meats

SOUPS
To warm your cold, bitter soul

How in this day and age can people still eat canned/carton soup? Making soup is literally child's play, making it in a slow cooker is minimal effort and time- then freeze servings. A slow cooker is under $100 and will save you money and add years to your life in the end.

"HARD TO TELL IT'S HAM-LESS" SPLIT PEA SOUP

By adding cloves to split peas, water, or broth and veggies you're creating a fat-free, high fiber and cholesterol-lowering soup. The cloves give the soup a wonderful flavor that imitates that of adding fat and sodium-loaded ham bone, so eat up lard ass.

Mirepoix
2 cartons or 8 cups of broth of choice (vegetable or chicken recommended) or water
1 pound of dried split peas, rinsed
3-4 whole cloves

Stovetop Option- Sauté the mirepoix in 2 tbs. of olive oil until soft
Add next 3 ingredients (liquid should be about ½ inch over peas) and bring to a boil
Lower to a simmer until peas are soft
Slow Cooker Option- add all ingredients together, cook 3 hours on high or 6 on low
Then (for both options)- Take a hand blender to the mixture and blend to a smooth consistency, if you don't have a hand blender you can transfer the mixture to a traditional blender.
If the consistency is too thick you can add water or broth to thin it out to desired consistency.

CHICKEN SOUP

STOP BUYING CANNED SOUP!
Read this and do it instead.

Mirepoix
3-4 thick-cut breasts, rinse & leave whole
3 cartons of chicken broth or 12 cups of homemade broth
Italian parsley

Stovetop Option- Sauté the mirepoix in 2 tbs. of olive oil until soft
Add next 3 ingredients
Boil until chicken is cooked
Slow Cooker Option- add all ingredients together, cook 3 hours on high or 6 on low
Then (for both options)- Take out cooked breasts and shred with a fork or cube them into bite-size pieces
Throw chicken back to soup vessel and EAT!

Freeze in individual portions and for the love of god STOP WITH THE F'ING PRESERVATIVES

For a one bowl, filling meal, make rice, a grain, or pasta to serve with the soup, just don't store it together- keep it separate until eating because the starchy stuff tends to soak up the precious broth.

"CREAM-LESS" CREAM OF BROCCOLI SOUP

Mirepoix
2 bags of organic frozen broccoli
2 cartons or 8 cups of broth of choice (vegetable or chicken recommended) or water
½ cup Cashew cream

Stovetop Option- Sauté the mirepoix in 2 tbs. olive oil until soft
Add next 2 ingredients
Bring to a boil, cook until broccoli is very tender
Slow Cooker Option- add all ingredients together, cook 4 hours on high or 8 on low
Then (for both options)- Puree with a hand blender or add all ingredients to a blender or processer with the cashew cream

"CREAM-LESS" CREAM OF TOMATO SOUP

Poix
2 cans of organic tomatoes, whole peeled or crushed (spring for the San Marzano)
2 cartons or 8 cups of broth of choice (vegetable or chicken recommended) or water
½ cup Cashew cream

Stovetop Option- Sauté the poix in 2 tbs. olive oil until soft
Add next 2 ingredients
Bring to a boil, cook until tomatoes are tender
Slow Cooker Option- add all ingredients together, cook 4 hours on high or 8 on low
Then (for both options)- Puree with a hand blender or add all ingredients to a blender or processer with the cashew cream

It's That easy!!!! So ENJOY MOFO!

VERSITAILE MINESTRONE IN MINUTES

How hard is it to eat your damn vegetables? Does everything you put into your poor body have to be from some poor, innocent animal? You can get plenty of protein from veggies and fill up easily without having digestion issues, other than a satisfying fart!
This soup can be done in such a wide array of fashions that it's almost impossible to make a standard recipe and it's impossible to not have it tailored to your liking. The basic rule for this soup is the tomato base, a bean for protein, any amount and/or a variety of vegetables, and a whole grain or pasta if you want a filling one-bowl meal.

I will give you a basic example recipe; it's low fat, full of fiber and nutrients. I like to always make huge batches of this and have individual servings in the freezer for quick one-bowl meals.

Mirepoix
1 24-ounce can of chopped tomatoes or if you have tomatoes going bad, chop them up and use that, a can of crushed tomatoes works as well
1 14-ounce can of organic tomato sauce or a small can of tomato paste
2 cartons or 8 cups of broth of choice (vegetable or chicken recommended) or water
Any and all choices of packaged frozen (efficient AF) or fresh veggies: chopped broccoli, spinach, squash, corn,

peppers, etc. I always like a leafy green like spinach to boost up the soup- spinach is easy, but play around with others, escarole is another favorite.
1 16-ounce can of beans of your choice (Protein, yo!)
1 cup of chosen carb (farro, brown rice, barley, pasta, etc.)

Stovetop Option- Sauté the mirepoix in 2 tbs. olive oil until soft
Add next 3 ingredients
Bring to a boil and add veggies
Once veggies are cooked tender, add the beans and let simmer until beans are soft
Slow Cooker Option- add all ingredients together except the grain, cook 4 hours on high or 8 on low
Then (for both options)- In a separate saucepan cook the grain of your choice according to package directions
When the grain is cooked you should stir in a little bit of oil or ladle some of the soup broth into it so that it does not stick
Combine soup and grain in your serving bowl and top with grated cheese, nutritional yeast, flavored herb oils, or hot sauce and MANGIA!

Keep the grain separate when storing leftovers, because if you package it together, it will soak up all of your precious broth and now you have vegetable stew

ITALIAN WEDDING SOUP

I like to use escarole as my veggie here, but if you want to use spinach or any other leafy green here that works fine, just add a veggie and please, for the love of god-f'ing eat it. This soup is the best example of a one-bowl meal, you have vegetables, a carbohydrate, and a protein, it's essentially a perfect meal for your imperfect body.

The soup:
2 tbs. olive oil
Poix
2 cartons or 8 cups of broth of choice (vegetable or chicken recommended) or water
1 bunch of escarole, washed well and torn into bite-sized pieces
1 16-ounce can of cannellini beans or great northern beans

The meatballs:
1 pound of ground turkey, chicken, beef, or vegetable protein "ground beef"
¼ cup of flat-leaf (Italian) parsley rinsed and picked off the stems
1 cup grated Romano cheese
1 cup of plain breadcrumbs
2 large eggs

Sauté poix in olive oil until soft

Add broth and escarole and cover
Bring to a boil- meanwhile make the meatballs:
Add all meatball ingredients in a bowl and using your fingers blend it all well together
Roll into about 1-inch diameter balls
Add all meatballs at once to the boiling soup pot as well as the beans
Cook until the meatballs are cooked through (7-10 mins)

Serve with grated Romano cheese if desired

LOW EFFORT LENTIL

If you're not eating lentils on rotation, why the hell not? They are essentially the perfect food- A half-cup of lentils has 115 calories, 7 grams of fiber, and 9 grams of protein- a nutritional powerhouse!!!!

Mirepoix
2 cartons or 8 cups of broth of choice (vegetable or chicken recommended) or water
1-pound bag of brown, black, green, or red OR a combo of colored lentils
1 12-ounce can of organic tomato sauce or a small can of tomato paste
½ a bag of frozen spinach

Stovetop Option- Sauté the mirepoix in 2 tbs. olive oil until soft
Add all the remaining ingredients
Bring to a boil, cook until lentils are tender
Slow Cooker Option- add all ingredients together, cook 4 hours on high or 8 on low

SEAFOOD BISQUE

Poix
2-3 Shallots
¼ cup of sherry wine or brandy
Small can tomato paste
1 cup cashew cream
2 cartons or 8 cups of seafood stock or vegetable broth or water
½ lb. raw, cleaned shrimp, deshelled, deveined, and cut into small pieces
1 can of cooked crab meat

Sauté first 2 items in olive oil or a pat or 2 of butter
Add liquor (careful now) cook off a few mins
Add next three ingredients and bring to a boil
Add shrimp, once pink add crab
Top with parsley and serve

"CREAM-LESS" CREAMY BUTTERNUT SQUASH SOUP

This soup is easy, very filling, and nutritious. I add Yams for even more filling fiber. It's so great to make because all of the ingredients can roast together in the oven leaving you with free time to jerk off.

1 large butternut squash or 2 smalls. Half them, scoop out seeds with a spoon, rinse & pierce with a fork in a few spots.
2 large Yams cut in half
Mirepoix
2 cartons or 8 cups of broth of choice (vegetable or chicken recommended) or water
1 tablespoon of honey or pure maple syrup (if you desire a sweeter soup)

Preheat the oven to 350-degrees
Spray a sheet pan with olive oil cooking spray and place halved squashes and yams face down on the sheet pan (lazy tip- line sheet with parchment paper or foil before spraying so you don't have to scrub that shit later)
Sprinkle with mirepoix and cover with foil
Cook for one hour or until a fork goes through the thickest part with total ease
Allow cooling until cool enough to touch
Using a spoon scoop out the flesh from squash and potatoes, add to a blender along with cooked mirepoix, add broth and honey or syrup, and puree until smooth

Pour mixture into a saucepan and heat on low heat until consumption time
If the mixture is too thick add broth or water to thin it out

Additional Options:
If you want to make it even sweeter because you're a fatty, you can add 1 tablespoon of brown sugar
Or if you fancy, to give it a more unique flavor add 1 teaspoon of pumpkin pie spice
Or add some roasted pumpkin seeds before serving if you're one of those protein heads

DETOX GINGER LEMONGRASS MUSHROOM SOUP

For you partiers who try to act all holy Monday through Thursday, juicing, gym-ing and shit, this should help undo some of the damage.

1 Tbs. sesame oil
Poix
1 Tbs. Umami (mushroom seasoning, doofus)
2 cups of mushroom of choice
4 cups of water or mushroom broth (if water is used, add more umami for a stronger mushroom flavor)
2-3 Serrano peppers (if you're a puss wuss and can't handle the heat, just omit it)
Freshly grated ginger
1 piece lemongrass
Scallions or green onion, whatever the F you call it

Sauté the first 3 ingredients until soft
Add next 5 ingredients and bring to a boil
Top with scallions and mow

CLAM CHOWDAH

Sooooo filling and light, I make the NE with cashew cream. Try making both and mixing them together for a Long Island Chowder.

MANHATTAN (RED)

Mirepoix
1 Shallot, chopped
Olive oil
1 Bottle of good quality clam juice
2 cups of seafood stock, vegetable broth, or water
6 oz. can tomato paste
6 medium red potatoes cut into bite-sized pieces
A hand full of fresh flat-leaf parsley
A dozen clams of choice (I like Little Necks)

Put the clams in a bowl of water in the fridge with cornmeal for at least an hour- this makes them spit out sand

Sauté the first 3 ingredients
Add clam juice, stock/broth/water, tomato, potatoes, and parsley, bring to a boil

Meanwhile, in a separate pot bring 2 cups of filtered water and bring to a boil
Rinse clams individually under vigorously running cold water

Add clams to boiling water, using a slotted spoon and turn the clams over and over until they open up as they open remove the clams and put them in a bowl
Once all clams are open (if one doesn't open- throw it out, it's dead and unsafe to eat) take them out of the shell and place them aside
Take the left-over water from steaming the clams and the bowl you pulled them aside in and strain thru a cheesecloth or a paper coffee filter to get any remaining sand out, reserve the liquid.

Add the liquid from the clams to the soup, boiling until potatoes are soft
Chop the clams or cut up with a scissor, combine altogether and enjoy

NEW ENGLAND (WHITE)

Do everything above- except- trade tomato paste for 1 cup cashew cream.

Save the clam and shrimp shells in the freezer to make more seafood stock later.

DATE NIGHT SOUP

Whenever my husband and I have plans to go out sans kid, I still have to feed the 'lil bugger. I really try to stay away from the nuggets and mac & cheese, because ya know, PRESERVATIVES!
This soup is done in minutes, has never been turned down by any kid or adult I know, and is another one-bowl meal.

2 tbs. olive oil
Mirepoix
2 cartons or 8 cups of chicken broth
1/2 bag frozen spinach
1 package of tortellini with cheese- NOT meat (you don't know what they put in there)

Sauté mirepoix in olive oil
Add broth & spinach bring to boil
Add tortellini, boil until soft
Grated cheese, BAM!

SAUCES
Because jarred sauce is for HACKS

BASIC POMODORO SAUCE (IT'S SAUCE, NOT GRAVY- GRAVY IS BROWN) & MEATBALLS

Still eating pre-made sauce? This takes 30 minutes so get a grip and stop with the damn preservatives. One to two cans per lb. of pasta.

5 cloves of garlic
2 tablespoons of olive oil
1 16 oz. can of whole peeled tomatoes if you like chunky or crushed tomatoes if you like smooth
1 tsp sugar
Fresh basil

Peel garlic cloves and cut into big chunks, add to a saucepan with olive oil
Remove the pan from heat when they just start to sizzle, once it stops sizzling, repeat step- you don't want the garlic to burn- if it does- start over
Add tomatoes and sugar and cover over medium heat
Once it comes to a boil, remove the cover and reduce to a simmer
Stir frequently to release water
If whole tomatoes are used, smash the tomatoes on the side of the saucepan while stirring as they cook, smash the garlic on the side as well as it softens
The sauce will cook for about 20-30 minutes to a thick consistency. Add basil leaves and serve.
Your sauce should be RED, NOT MAROON, NOT PURPLE- Bright f'ing RED

* If you're making a sauce for meatballs add one whole, peeled onion pierced with 5-8 whole cloves to the saucepan as the sauce cooks, remove before serving.

The meatballs:
1 pound of ground turkey, chicken, beef, or vegetable protein "ground beef"
¼ cup of flat-leaf (Italian) parsley rinsed and picked off the stems
1 cup grated Romano cheese
1 cup of plain breadcrumbs
2 large eggs

Add all ingredients to a bowl and using your fingers blend it all well together
Roll into about 3-inch diameter balls
Bake or air fry at 375-degrees for 20 mins on a sheet pan OR Fry in olive oil until they are brown on all sides
Add all at once to your cooking sauce pot
Cook until the meatballs are cooked through (7-10 mins)
Serve with grated Romano cheese if desired

ALA VODKA

2-3 large shallots, finely chopped
2 tablespoons of olive oil
1 cup of vodka
2 cups of basic Pomodoro (recipe on the previous page)
1 cup of grated Romano cheese
1 cup of cashew cream

Sauté shallots in olive oil over medium heat, stirring frequently until they are soft and translucent (about 8 minutes) don't let burn
Add vodka (carefully away from flames) and cook about 3-4 minutes more until the alcohol has cooked down
Add tomato sauce and cook about 5 minutes more
Add the grated cheese and cashew cream and stir well until you get a pinkish color (sauce will be thick) stir well

Make 1 pound of pasta according to package directions while making the sauce. Once cooked add the pasta to the sauce instead of topping the pasta with the sauce because the sauce is thick and needs to coat the pasta. Stir to coat it all and serve right away.

PUMPKIN SAUCE PASTA

1 large shallot, chopped
1 Tablespoon olive oil
1 16-ounce can organic puree of butternut squash
1 16-ounce can organic puree of pumpkin
2 cartons or 8 cups of broth of choice (vegetable or chicken recommended) or water
¼ cup grated Romano cheese
2 Tbs fresh sage
½ cup of toasted, unsalted, chopped pecans

Sauté the shallot in olive oil until very soft and almost translucent
Add squash, pumpkin, and broth and bring to a boil
Once it boils, lower it to a simmer and add sage
Cook for 20 minutes, occasionally stirring

Make 1 pound of pasta according to package directions while making the sauce. Once cooked add the pasta to the sauce instead of topping the pasta with the sauce because the sauce is thick and needs to coat the pasta. Stir to coat it while adding the Romano and serve right away.

Top with pecans if desired.

CLAM SAUCE

For the love of god- please don't use canned clams- fresh is easy and (unless you live in the boonies) you should be able to buy fresh clams for a few bucks. I prefer Little Neck, but any species of clam will do- freshness is the most important aspect.

1 large head of garlic- peeled and chopped
¼ cup olive oil
Fresh Italian flat-leaf parsley, trimmed and roughly chopped
1 bottle of high-quality clam juice (buy the bottled one)
12-24 clams of choice (figure 6 clams per person average)

Put the clams in a bowl of water in the fridge with cornmeal for at least an hour- this makes them spit out sand
Bring 1-2 cups of water to a boil in a pot that will be large enough to hold the clams
Rinse clams individually under vigorously running cold water
Add clams to boiling water, use a slotted spoon and turn the clams over and over until they open up as they open remove the clams and put them in a colander atop a bowl

Once all clams are open (if one doesn't open- throw it out, it's dead and unsafe to eat) take them out of the shell and place them aside
Take the left-over water from steaming the clams and the liquid in the bowl from under the colander and strain thru a cheesecloth or a paper coffee filter to get any remaining sand out, reserve the liquid
In a large pan sauté the garlic in olive oil
Add parsley, reserved clam cooking water, and bottled clam juice, and cook some more
Add clams to the pan, cook 1-2 mins more, and serve on top of spaghetti or linguine

Save the shells in the freezer to make seafood stock later

MAINS WITH GRAINS

RISOTTO WITH MUSHROOMS

The key to a good risotto is to stir, stir, stir, low and slow, it's the absorption of liquid that infuses the flavor. Feel free to sub the mushrooms with your favorite vegetable, any will do.

1 yellow onion finely chopped
1 tablespoon olive oil
½ cup of dry white wine
1 cup of organic rice (short grain is best, particularly Arborio, but any rice works here)
1 package of fresh mushrooms of choice (I like baby Bella's)
Liquid of choice- chicken, vegetable broth, or water as needed (about 4 cups)
½ cup of grated Romano cheese
Sprinkle of thyme

Using a large sauté pan, sauté the onion in olive oil until soft
Add wine, cook 5 mins
Add rice and coat in onion/wine mixture about 5 mins
Add 1 cup of vegetable broth at a time, stir it in, as it gets absorbed add another cup at a time allowing it to absorb until rice is soft and cooked
Add the mushrooms and cook until soft
Add cheese and thyme
Serve immediately very hot

If you fancy, top with truffle oil before serving
If you bougie, shave some fresh truffles on top

ROASTED CAULIFLOWER AND/OR BROCCOLI WITH CANELLINI BEANS OVER PASTA

One bowl meal bitches! If you must have meat, you can add or sub out the beans for sausages and cook the same way.

1 large head cauliflower and/or broccoli, washed and cut into bite-size pieces, or use bags of frozen florets
2 Tbs olive oil
6 cloves of garlic
1 16-ounce can of cannellini beans rinsed and drained well
1 large onion, finely chopped

Pre-heat oven to 375-degrees
Spray a baking dish with olive oil spray and add cauliflower, oil, garlic, beans, onions
Cover with foil and bake/roast for 30 minutes
Meanwhile, boil water for the pasta and when 10 minutes are left on the timer for the veggie/bean thing, add the pasta to the boiling water and cook according to package directions
Also at this time remove the foil on the veg/bean, this will allow it to brown a bit
Drain pasta well and combine the pasta with the cauliflower mixture, drizzle olive oil on top

PAELLA
This is a one-bowl meal, dinner party hit, this recipe serves 4-6 people

I traditionally make straight-up seafood only paella, you can add chorizo sliced in rounds and chicken chunks, as well as use chicken stock if you would like a more traditional dish. I also steam my shellfish open in a separate vessel because I once had a clam spew black sludge and ruin the precious broth I was creating, so excuse the extra step.

2 Tbs olive oil
6 cloves of garlic, chopped finely
1 large Spanish onion, chopped
1 bell pepper, diced
1 cup dry white wine
3 cups of short-grain rice (Arborio)
Liquid of choice- chicken, vegetable stock, or water as needed (about 4 cups) I use seafood stock
1 tsp. saffron threads
14 ounce can chop tomatoes, or 2-3 diced plum tomatoes
½ cup flat-leaf parsley
Bag of frozen peas
Seafood of choice- I do a dozen Little Neck clams, 2 dozen mussels, 1 pound of shrimp (cleaned, deveined, and tail on or off, doesn't matter)

Put the clams & mussels in a bowl of water in the fridge with cornmeal for at least an hour- this makes them spit out sand

In a large Dutch oven or saucepan, sauté onions and garlic in olive oil until soft

Add bell pepper and cook, stirring until soft

Add wine and cook down a bit

Add rice, stock, saffron, tomatoes, ½ the parsley and cover to a boil

Once boiling add peas and lower to a simmer

Meanwhile, in a separate saucepan bring 1-2 cups of water to a boil in a pot

Rinse clams & mussels individually under vigorously running cold water

Add clams to boiling water, use a slotted spoon and turn the clams over and over until they open up as they open remove the clams and put in a colander atop a bowl to catch the liquid, repeat with mussels, using the same boiling water

Once all clams & mussels are open (if one doesn't open- throw it out, it's dead and unsafe to eat) leave them in the shell, just set aside

Take the left-over water from steaming the clams & mussels and the colander bowl, strain thru a cheesecloth or a paper coffee filter to get any remaining sand out, reserve the liquid

Make sure the rice is soft, add the liquid from the shellfish boil as needed, and stir

Once the rice is soft add raw shrimp and stir until curled and pink, add clams and mussels in the shell to the rice mixture
Stir all together for a minute or 2 to mix together ingredients, add liquid as needed using shellfish liquid
Sprinkle remaining parsley on top and serve

MEATY MAINS

Eat meat sparingly if you must eat it, poor, beautiful animals have to spare their lives for your fat ass

ESCAROLE AND BEANS WITH SAUSAGE

Another one-bowl meal, bitches!

1 Tbs olive oil
5 garlic cloves
1 yellow onion, sliced
1-2 large bunches of fresh escarole, rinsed very well and torn into pieces
1 16-oz can of cannellini beans, not drained
1 package of turkey sausage, chicken sausage, or meatless sausage

Sauté garlic and onion in olive oil until soft
Add escarole, add a little water or broth and cover 15 mins, add more liquid if needed
Add beans with liquid cook 5 minutes more
Slice the sausages, brown in a separate frying pan quick
Add to the escarole
Cook until sausage is cooked through
Serve with grated cheese and crushed red pepper

CHICKEN A FEW WAYS

Because these days no bird is safe in most people's wakes- Buy thick breasts and do this:

Rinse the breasts and add to a cooking vessel of choice and add:

For 3 breasts-
½ cup balsamic vinegar
¼ cup olive oil
1 tablespoon Italian seasoning
OR
A packet of taco seasoning
Once cooked, shred with a fork
Serve with taco accouterments
OR
Your favorite marinade
Serve over mashed cauliflower with a green vegetable for a guilt-free, well-rounded meal

Oven Option- Cook on a foil, oil lined sheet pan at 400-degrees for 20-25 minutes (depending on thickness, 165-degree interior temperature or until there is no pink center)
Slow Cooker Option- Low 6 hours, high 3

CHICKEN CUTLETS

These are so easy to make, SO stop buying the deep-fried premade ones for heaven's sake

Chicken breasts
1 cup of breadcrumbs
½ cup grated cheese
½ tsp. Italian Seasoning
2 eggs

Wash and pat dry the chicken, slice lengthwise in half if you prefer thin
Combine the next 3 ingredients in one bowl
Whisk eggs in another bowl, then, I don't know who need to hear this but (insert eye roll) dip the cutlets in the egg mixture and then immediately coat the cutlet in the breadcrumb mixture

Transfer to the sheet pan that has been sprayed with cooking spray or lightly greased
Bake or air fry for approximately 20 minutes- depending on thickness will determine cooking time, turn them over ½ way through and make sure there is no pink anywhere

Serve with marinara for dipping or squeeze of lemon juice or make a quick tomato salad and top the cutlets with that (chopped tomatoes, olive oil, basil) for Milanese style

THE BEST DAMN SHRIMP EVA!!!!

Keep bags of raw & cleaned frozen shrimp in the freezer for quick low-cal meals. They defrost in minutes and are so versatile.

½ lb. frozen shrimp or about 2 cups
½ cup sesame oil
6 cloves garlic (crushed)
¼ cup cilantro chopped
Few dashes of hot sauce
¼ cup lime juice

Put shrimp in a bowl of cold water to defrost, change the water every 10 mins as you prepare the marinade
Combine next 5 ingredients
Marinate shrimp in the concoction for as long as you can in the fridge
Options:
Sauté shrimp with marinade, when they turn pink and curl, they are done- serve over rice.
Skewer shrimp and grill or broil, cook marinade in a small saucepan, and pour over cooked skewers

ITALIAN TUNA

Lemon & oil vs. mayo....no brainer.

1 can of high-quality tuna fish packed in oil
1/2 sweet onion
1 Tbs. olive oil
¼ cup chopped celery
Juice of 1 lemon
¼ cup sliced black olives (optional)

Combine all ingredients together and mow up

CHILI

1 large white or yellow onion
1 tbs olive oil
1 each green and red bell pepper cut in bite-sized pieces
1 28 ounce can of organic tomato sauce
2 15oz. cans of red kidney beans or pinto beans or one of each
3 Tbs.-1/4 cup of chili powder depending on how spicy you like it
Tabasco sauce according to spice preference or hot pepper (such as one jalapeño chopped and added to pepper onion mixture)
1 lb. of ground meat of choice or omit the meat and add an extra can of beans for a vegetarian chili

Stovetop Option- Sauté the onions and peppers (or hack like I do and buy bags of frozen peppers & onions already cut and mixed) in olive oil until they are soft
Pour the tomato sauce, beans, and spices in the pot with the onions and bring to a slow boil
Meanwhile in a shallow frying pan heat the chopped meat and brown it, transfer the meat to a strainer and drain the extra grease
Add the meat to the sauce mixture and heat it all together at a simmer until meat is cooked through
Slow Cooker Option- add all ingredients together, cook 4 hours on high or 8 on low
Serve with shredded cheddar and sour cream

PULLED CHICKEN OR PORK

If you must eat pork, but know that pigs are 50x smarter than dogs so get one as a pet and stop clogging your arteries with its brilliant flesh!

Thick-cut chicken breasts or a pork butt or shoulder
Make a rub- Mix 1 tbsp each brown sugar, garlic powder, paprika, chili powder
2 white or yellow onions, sliced in 1/4" rings
BBQ Sauce (if desired)

Line the bottom of your slow cooker or roasting pan with your onion rings
Rinse and pat meat dry
Use hand to get rub all over the meat
Place on onions
Oven Option- Cook at 300-degrees for 3 hours covered
Cook one hour more uncovered (for approx. 4lb of meat)
Slow Cooker Option-
Low 8 hours, high 4
Then (for both options)- Shred meat with a fork and add back in with the natural juices and onions, mix
Serve with BBQ sauce, sweet rolls & a type of slaw if desired

VEGGIE MAINS

EGGPLANT

Enjoy eggplant in a non-parmesan way for once, fatty

1 large eggplant
4 cloves of garlic in large pieces
1 28 oz. can of chopped tomatoes
Fresh basil leaves
Grated cheese or part-skim mozzarella

Cut eggplant in 1/4" circles (peel the skin if preferred) and salt the rounds with Kosher salt, cover with a kitchen towel and let drain to get out water for 30 minutes to an hour
Brush off the salt from eggplant, brush pieces with olive oil
Broil each side for 5-7 mins
Preheat the oven to 375- degrees and spray a baking dish with olive oil spray
Place eggplant in a baking dish in an overlapping pattern
Cover the eggplant with the tomatoes, sprinkle some chopped basil, the garlic, and cover with foil
Bake for 30 minutes and uncover and top with cheese, bake for 15 minutes more and sprinkle with more basil before you serve

ZUCCHINI OR EGGPLANT LASAGNA

A low-carb, delicious, baked dish that feels like you're eating lasagna! This is one of those dishes that tastes even better the next day because it has time to settle and meld, so it's a great make-ahead dish you can eat all week or serve to a crowd.

8 medium-sized zucchinis or 3 large eggplants
½ cup to ¾ cup of grated Romano cheese
2 cups of Pomodoro sauce
1 cup of ricotta cheese
1 cup of shredded mozzarella for topping

Slice zucchini/ep lengthwise (thin to win) use a mandolin slicer so that you get even pieces for primal layering
Salt the rounds with Kosher salt, cover with a kitchen towel, and let drain to get out water for 30 minutes to an hour
Brush each piece with olive oil and broil until soft on both sides
Take a 9" baking dish and layer like this- sauce, zuc/ep, spread the 3 cheeses until you use all veggies
Top with sauce and mozz, spray foil with olive oil, and cover- bake for at least an hour at 375-degrees
IMPOSSIBLE TO OVERCOOK
Take off foil and let the cheese brown a bit under the broiler- serve with sauce and grated cheese

CURRY IN A HURRY
UGH- Did I just say that!?!?!?!?

Mire Poix
4 heads garlic
3-4 tsp. each ginger & cilantro (I use frozen cubes of fresh ones that I buy in the freezer from the produce dept.)
13.5 oz. can of full-fat coconut milk
16 oz. can have chopped tomatoes
3-4 tbs. curry powder
1 tbs. each coriander, cumin, chili powder
2-3 bay leaf
1 tbs. red pepper or something spicy, hot sauce, chipotle peppers, etc. (if you like spicy)
Veggies- frozen or fresh about 1-2 cups each of spinach, broccoli, cauliflower, cubed sweet or white potatoes - you decide
1 can chickpeas
Optional- cubed chicken breast meat or tofu

Stovetop Option- Sauté the mirepoix and garlic in 2 tbs. of coconut or avocado oil until soft
Add the rest of the ingredients
Bring to a boil then lower to a simmer
When vegetables are tender add tofu/chicken
Cook until tofu/chicken is cooked
Slow Cooker Option- add all ingredients together, cook 3 hours on high or 6 on low

Then (for both options) - Make Basmati rice for a one-bowl meal

STEWS
To stick to the ribs you haven't felt since High School

BEEF STEW

Mirepoix
1-cup tomato sauce
Carton of beef broth
3 bay leaves
¼ cup Worchester Sauce
1 cup of red wine
1 lb. red or yellow potatoes cut into chunks (skin on)
2 lbs. of beef for stew (chuck or round)

TURKEY OR CHICKEN STEW

Mirepoix
Carton of chicken broth
3 bay leaves
1 lb. red or yellow potatoes cut into chunks (skin on)
¼ cup Worchester Sauce
1 cup of Dry White Wine
2 lbs. of turkey or chicken breasts

Trim fat on meat and cut into 1-inch squares
In a frying pan- just brown the outside of the meat squares in light olive oil and set them aside on a paper towel-lined plate, then:
Oven Option- Sauté the mirepoix in 2 tbs. olive oil until soft add all ingredients to a heavy roasting pan/Dutch oven and roast or bake on 325-degrees for about 90 minutes until potatoes are soft

Slow Cooker Option - add all ingredients together, cook 4 hours on high or 8 on low

WHITE BEAN STEW WITH SAUSAGE AND SPINACH

Poix
Olive Oil
2 15oz. can of cannellini or white kidney beans (drain/rinse 1 can only)
Bag of fresh or frozen spinach
Sausage of choice (I use veggie ones)

Sauté poix in oil
Add all beans and liquid from the can- cook 5 mins, smash some on the side (1/4 of them)
Add spinach, then cover and cook on medium heat until soft and hot (10-15 mins)
Slice sausages in rounds and separately dry pan fry each side until both sides are browned, serve together

VEGETABLES/SIDES
Eat your damn greens

CREAM "LESS" CREAMED SPINACH OR CORN

1 large shallot, chopped
1 Tablespoon olive oil
1 cup cashew cream
2 cans of corn or 6 ears of fresh corn, niblets cut off and boiled for 10 minutes
Or
1 lb. of fresh, washed, de-stemmed, or frozen spinach

Chop and sauté the shallot in olive oil until very soft and almost translucent
Add corn or spinach
Add cashew cream and cook down about 3-4 minutes stirring frequently
Reduce to low heat and stirring randomly, allowing the cream to permeate the vegetable, about 30-45 minutes

ROASTED BRUSSELS

The trick here is to cut the butts off the sprout, cut an X into the bottom and soak in cold, salted water for at least an hour, it reduces bitterness

Brussels
Olive oil
1 large yellow onion chopped

Preheat oven to 4000-degrees
Rinse salted sprouts
Add all to a sheet pan
Drizzle with oil and roast for 30-40 mins uncovered

BUTTERNUT SQUASH PUREE

2 large butternut squash, rinsed, halved, and seeded
1 lb. bag of baby carrots
1-2 cups vegetable broth OR ½ cup cashew cream

Preheat oven to 375-degrees
Spray a sheet pan with cooking spray and lay the squash face side down surround by the baby carrots
Peirce squash skin with a fork in a few spots
Cover with foil
Bake for approximately 45 minutes or until a fork goes thru the thickest part of the squash with ease

Take out and let it cool
Scoop out the flesh of the squash add directly to a processor or blender along with the carrots

Here is where the recipe can vary:
For creamy (like mashed potato consistency) add cashew cream
For lighter variation add vegetable broth until you reach the desired consistency

GREEK OR ITALIAN STYLE GRAIN OR PASTA SALAD

Make this instead of fattening potato and macaroni salad, which really is ill-suited if you think about it- mayonnaise-laden carbs sitting in the blazing sun at the BBQ- gross!

2 cups of whole-wheat couscous, quinoa, whole-wheat orzo, brown rice, or a mixture of any of these whole grains or pasta of choice
1 tsp dried or fresh dill
1 tsp dried or fresh Italian or Greek oregano
¼ cup red onion finely chopped
½ cup pitted Kalamata olives chopped or whole (depends on your preference)
½ cup of grape tomatoes halved
½ cup chopped cucumber
¼ cup chopped toasted walnuts (to toast raw walnuts place on a cookie sheet in a preheated 375-degree oven for 8 minutes)
1 Tablespoon of walnut, avocado, or olive oil
½ cup feta cheese
1 cup of vegetable broth or more if needed to moisten grains

Cook grain/s of choice according to package direction, omitting butter if stated
Place cooked grains in a bowl, add oil and broth, stir well and allow it to cool (put in the fridge if time is of the essence)

Once cooled add herbs, onion, tomato, cucumbers & olives
Leave out to room temperature
Add feta & walnuts and serve

A variation on the recipe for **ITALIAN GRAIN SALAD**:

Use olive oil
Replace feta with part-skim mozzarella
Replace dill & oregano with chopped fresh basil
Replace walnuts with pine nuts

ITALIAN POTATO SALAD

If you must have it, do this! So much lighter than American style and that mayo in the sun thing.

1 lb. of red-skinned potatoes, eastern potatoes, or Yukon's
2 Tbs. of <u>fresh</u> Italian oregano (not pizza parlor oregano)
½ cup chopped red onion
1 Tbs olive oil
½ cup chopped black olives
½ cup chopped celery
3 Tbs lemon juice

Soak raw potatoes in salted water for 20 minutes to loosen dirt
Meanwhile, fill a stockpot with water and bring it to a boil
Scrub, rinse, and cut the potatoes (bite-size)
Add to boiling water and boil for approximately 15 minutes or until a fork goes thru a piece with ease
Drain and toss with olive oil
Place in the fridge to cool
Once cool (approximately 30 minutes) add the remaining ingredients, mix well, and serve at room temperature

ONE SWEET TREAT
Because your fat ass must have some sugar

THE GO-TO DESSERT

This is not a book about throwing a dinner party or whatever- but I will share my one go-to dessert in a pinch. Everyone has fruit on hand, yes? Apples, bananas, oranges- whatever fruit you go with just stick with it. Don't combine fruits.

Slice fruit into reasonably sized pieces
Sauté fruit in a pat or 2 of butter, sprinkle some cinnamon and cook down until fruit's soft
Melt ½ stick butter, add ½ cup flour of choice, 1 tsp. cinnamon and ½ cup sugar or brown sugar even better- mix until you get a crumb-like consistency- think coffee cake crumbs

Put vanilla ice cream in individual portion bowls, top with Sautéed fruit and crumbs

You're welcome

KITCHEN HACKS
Good learned shit here…..

- Replacing mayo with straight-up avocado (dash of lemon or lime juice if not eating right away so it doesn't turn brown) in most recipes works (egg salad, tuna salad, etc.)
- Roast frozen veggies instead of boiling
- Freeze rotting bananas and use to sweeten recipes, or make "nice" cream (look it up)
- Shake garlic cloves in a mason jar to remove the skin easily
- Do not throw out that pickle juice! Use it as a brine for a meat marinade OR boil it and re-pickle any veg you want (onions, radishes, carrots, even hard-boiled eggs) OR do a Pickle-back shot with it- Look it up!
- Make protein pancakes for a healthy breakfast- blend one banana and 2 eggs to make the batter and cook like a regular pancake
- Pre-make little omelets for quick on the go breakfasts- spray/grease muffin tin really well, add veggies, meats, cheeses to each cup, make a variety, pour egg whites or beaten eggs over, bake at 350-degrees for 20 mins
- Roll citrus fruits before cutting for maximum juice extraction
- Make your own oat milk- soak oats overnight in water, drain and blend with filtered water, strain

chunks out and the reserved liquid is what you are paying top dollar for, make cookies, dog treats, or overnight oats with the leftover oats
- Ripen produce on the counter, once ripe place in the fridge to cease ripening
- Buy the frozen herb cubes for maximum efficiency